# Including young people in urban regeneration

## A lot to learn?

Suzanne Fitzpatrick, Annette Hastings and Keith Kintrea

**The POLICY PRESS**

First published in Great Britain in 1998 by

The Policy Press
University of Bristol
Rodney Lodge
Grange Road
Bristol BS8 4EA
UK

Tel      +44 (0)117 973 8797
Fax      +44 (0)117 973 7308
E-mail  tpp@bristol.ac.uk
Website http://www.bristol.ac.uk/Publications/TPP

© The Policy Press and the Joseph Rowntree Foundation, 1998
In association with the Joseph Rowntree Foundation

ISBN 1 86134 119 9

Photographs used on the front cover were supplied by kind permission of John Birdsall Photography, Nottingham.

**Suzanne Fitzpatrick** is Research Fellow, **Annette Hastings** is Research Fellow and **Keith Kintrea** is Senior Lecturer in the Department of Urban Studies, University of Glasgow.

The **Joseph Rowntree Foundation** has supported this project as part of its programme of research and innovative development projects, which it hopes will be of value to policy makers and practitioners. The facts presented and the views expressed in this report, however, are those of the authors and not necessarily those of the Foundation.

The statements and opinions contained within this publication are solely those of the authors and contributors and not of The University of Bristol or The Policy Press. The University of Bristol and The Policy Press disclaim responsibility for any injury to persons or property resulting from any material published in this publication.

The Policy Press works to counter discrimination on grounds of gender, race, disability, age and sexuality.

Cover design by Qube Design Associates, Bristol.
Printed in Great Britain by Hobbs the Printers Ltd, Southampton.

# Contents

# Acknowledgements

We would like to thank all the young people, staff of local authorities and other agencies, elected members and community representatives who participated in the research. We are especially grateful to those people in six of the case studies who we interviewed on two separate occasions. We also thank the Joseph Rowntree Foundation, which funded this project within its Area Regeneration Programme, especially John Low, the Project Manager for the Foundation. The Project Advisory Group provided constructive advice and guidance throughout the project. Its members were:

Alan Barr, Scottish Community Development Centre and Department of Social Policy, University of Glasgow

Austen Cutten, The Pan London Community Regeneration Consortium

Sandra Davidson, Castlemilk Youth Complex, Glasgow

Mary Durkin, Camden Youth Service, formerly of the National Youth Agency

Barbara Lally, Gateshead Young Women's Project

Justin Plaskett, *The Big Issue* Cymru

John Tibbett, Education and Industry Department, The Scottish Office

# Summary

Youth issues have gained prominence within area-based regeneration initiatives since the early 1990s as the difficulties faced by young people living within disadvantaged communities have become increasingly apparent. This study set out to answer two questions:

- To what extent have young people's needs been addressed by urban regeneration initiatives and their projects and programmes?

- What is the nature and impact of young people's participation in decision making about urban regeneration?

The research involved detailed case studies of 12 urban regeneration initiatives across the UK. In total, over 200 people were interviewed in the course of the research, including more than 80 young people.

The research found that there were some important similarities in young people and adult decision makers' priorities for youth within regeneration, but also some striking contrasts. Both adults and young people stressed the need for youth employment and leisure opportunities. However, adults also emphasised young people's education and training needs, and were concerned to secure their involvement in the regeneration process. Young people, on the other hand, focused upon police harassment and changing adults' perceptions of their age group.

There was a wide range of projects aimed at young people within the case study initiatives. Economic projects which sought to link young people with existing job and training opportunities were almost universal. Education projects were also common, but most of these focused on under-16s. Projects which concerned housing and health were often either absent or very small scale, but some attention was given to providing leisure facilities for young people. Given young people's own self-defined needs, a significant gap in these programmes was projects which addressed their relationship with the police. Most projects seemed to have quite effectively targeted the more disadvantaged young people, but they were usually working with a narrow age range (14- to 19-year-olds). Disadvantaged young people in their 20s often seemed to be considered 'a lost cause'.

Youth forums were the most common mechanism used to facilitate youth involvement in regeneration. They provided a visible structure to facilitate ongoing participation by young people, and the youngest age groups preferred parallel youth structures, such as forums, to direct involvement in adult community groups. However, youth forums often lacked a sense of purpose; were not well-integrated with wider decision-making structures; and did not have a democratic and accountable structure. Some of these problems were attributable to the relatively new and experimental status of youth forums in the regeneration context. Youth forums seemed to work most effectively where they had a specific set of objectives, and where there was an opportunity for participants to have fun as well as to attend meetings. It is important for arrangements to be made for youth forums to regularly feed their views into the local regeneration initiative. The membership of youth forums generally reflected the local population of young people as regards ethnicity, gender and social background, and this was mainly due to the anti-discrimination ethic of youth workers.

There was a range of other mechanisms for involving young people employed in the case study initiatives including: youth conferences; focus group discussions; youth delegates on partnership boards and community forums; and delegated power given to youth groups over budgets or projects. Youth involvement was most effectively achieved by a combination of these methods so that as many young people as possible could have an opportunity to influence the regeneration process. It was also useful to find ways to bring young people and adults together to discuss issues affecting their community. However, some case studies showed that there was a danger that youth forums could become the only means to consult with young people in some areas.

It took far longer to build young people's capacity to participate than for adult community representatives because they were normally 'starting from scratch' with no previous involvement in community activism. This suggests that youth involvement projects have to be scheduled early in the life of an initiative if they are to make any real impact. The intensity of support needed to facilitate youth involvement is also greater than for equivalent adult structures. Therefore, substantial resources are required for effective youth participation, in particular the provision of dedicated workers is crucial. However, the funds allocated to most youth participation initiatives were small and insufficient to provide the support needed for effective involvement.

The study shows that successful youth involvement also requires the commitment of adults involved in regeneration initiatives. While most adults accepted the validity of involving young people in regeneration, there was a general lack of awareness about the changes which were often required in their working practices, language and behaviour in order to engage with young people.

The impacts of youth involvement on regeneration strategies and projects were minor and limited to youth-specific issues rather than matters affecting the community as a whole. However, the individual young people involved in initiatives have gained significant benefits, such as increased self-confidence and skills. Youth involvement has also had a very positive impact on the perceptions of councillors, officials and community activists about young people and their capacity to participate in decision making.

The study supports the value of including youth in regeneration, as a group whose welfare is critical to the future health of society. It is important that regeneration encompasses the needs expressed by young people and recognises the range of their material disadvantage. Youth-focused regeneration initiatives should be integrated as far as possible with other parts of a regeneration strategy and with mainstream services. There are strong signs that the Government has moved young people's needs up the agenda in its further support for youth-focused regeneration schemes in SRB4 (Single Regeneration Budget), in the New Deal and in its attention to education, all of which heightens the need to ensure effective coordination.

# Introduction

Since the early 1990s young people's needs and demands have become important concerns for regeneration initiatives. Drawing on the results of a major research study, this report suggests that, while substantial progress has been made in some areas, many adults still have a lot to learn about including youth in regeneration. The report considers the inclusion of young people aged 16-24 in urban regeneration initiatives: both the extent to which their needs have been addressed, and whether they have been engaged as active participants in regeneration decision making.

## The double disadvantage of youth

Young people have gradually become more disadvantaged relative to adults since the 1980s. This is the disadvantage of youth. Young people living in areas of multiple deprivation have suffered more acutely than young people living in other kinds of neighbourhoods. This is the double disadvantage faced by the groups of young people who are the focus of this report.

### Unemployment

Youth unemployment has grown dramatically since the 1970s, and has consistently outstripped adult rates. While youth unemployment fell in the mid-1990s, unemployment levels remain in excess of 30 % among the most disadvantaged young people in some deprived areas (Roberts, 1997).

### Lower wages

Youth incomes have declined considerably in real terms since the 1970s and the gap between adult wages and youth wages has widened. For example, in 1979 full-time male employees aged 16 and 17 earned around two thirds of the average full-time male wage, but by 1995 they earned only a third (Hickman, 1997).

### Reduced entitlement to benefit

Since 1988, 16- and 17-year-olds have not been entitled to Income Support, except in exceptional circumstances, and 18- to 24-year-olds have received lower rates than over-25s. Under-25s have also been impoverished by changes to the Housing Benefit system in 1988, with further restrictions implemented in 1996, and by the establishment of Job Seekers' Allowance in 1996.

### Higher levels of homelessness

Young people suffer disproportionately from homelessness. While 16- to 24-year-olds represent only 17% of the UK adult population, they comprise 25% of homeless applicants (Evans, 1996). The causes of youth homelessness include unemployment, poverty and family breakdown, as well as an insufficient supply of appropriate housing for young people, particularly young single people from disadvantaged communities.

### Increased health risks

Disadvantaged young people are more likely to be involved in activities such as smoking and 'hard' drug use which are a potential threat to their health (Furlong and Cartmel, 1997). Also, young people who feel vulnerable to unemployment are more prone to mental health problems (West and Sweeting, 1996).

*Lower rates of educational attainment*

Despite growing numbers of qualified school leavers and increasing rates of participation in post-compulsory education, strong distinctions remain in the levels of educational attainment of young people from different socioeconomic groups, particularly among the least qualified youth (Furlong and Cartmel, 1997).

*Greater risk of being a victim of crime*

Young people are more likely to be victims of personal, particularly violent, crime than adults. In 1996, almost 21% of men aged 16-25 reported being victims of violent crime, compared to 4% of men aged 26 and over (Black et al, 1996). Since people who live in disadvantaged areas are more likely to be victims of crime than those living elsewhere, young people within those areas are likely to be at special risk.

*Political marginalisation*

In addition to these social and economic disadvantages faced by many young people, there is a long-standing concern that this age group does not engage in the political process to the same extent as older adults. Disadvantaged young people are least likely to exercise their political rights, including voting. Attention has been focused on this political disenfranchisement with the growing national and international recognition of children's and young people's rights to participate in decisions which affect their lives. This philosophy is enshrined in the UN Convention of the Rights of the Child, ratified by the UK Government in 1991, and in the 1989 Children Act.

Young people living within disadvantaged communities therefore encounter a combination of economic, social and political problems which make their transition to adulthood very problematic (Furlong and Cartmel, 1997). While some observers have argued that a new 'underclass' of young people has emerged which rejects mainstream adult values, others argue that these young people should be considered 'socially excluded' by processes within wider society. The Cabinet Office Social Exclusion Unit has published reports on its two initial priorities, truancy and rough sleeping, and both are issues which particularly affect young

people. The third priority, 'worst estates', relates to the urban regeneration agenda which this report seeks to highlight.

# Urban regeneration and the emergence of a youth focus

Urban regeneration is a shorthand term to describe the process of renewal which is sought through policies, programmes and projects aimed at urban areas which have experienced industrial decline and/or multiple disadvantage. These areas may range from inner-city enclaves and self-contained housing estates on the urban periphery to whole towns and cities or even regions. Urban regeneration embodies both economic objectives, such as stimulating investment, and social objectives, such as alleviating the problems caused by poverty and disadvantage. Most conceptions of regeneration hold that economic and social problems are entwined and that regeneration will not be sustainable unless both aspects are tackled (DETR, 1997).

The larger regeneration initiatives originate with central Government. Throughout the 1980s and early 1990s a plethora of schemes and funding mechanisms existed, including the Urban Development Corporations and City Challenge. After 1994 regeneration budgets of four departments were rolled together into the Single Regeneration Budget Challenge Fund (SRB). In Scotland, the Government's flagship is the 'New Life' Urban Partnerships established in 1989. However, many local authorities have also sought to establish regeneration initiatives by prioritising budgets towards particular groups or areas, and local communities have also put together initiatives, by tapping into public, private and charitable funds. SRB schemes and the Scottish Priority Partnership Areas demand that local authorities, community groups and other agencies cooperate in partnerships in order to bid for a share of the available money.

Youth issues have gained prominence within urban regeneration initiatives since the early 1990s. This has arisen partly from an increased awareness of the problems endured by contemporary youth. However, the problems caused by young people have also been an important stimulus for the growth of a youth focus. There has been considerable political and media interest in something called the 'youth problem', with attention focused on vandalism, muggings and 'joy riding'. It is clear that aspects of some young people's behaviour does affect the quality of life enjoyed by other groups within communities. However, it has also been argued that the 'moral panics' about youth which have gripped the nation in recent years have been out of proportion to the actual level of problems.

The 'problematic' model of youth has undoubtedly informed Government policy. For example, the riots in the 1980s involving young people are credited with protecting the Urban Programme against substantial cuts and providing the impetus for the establishment of Task Forces in 1985 (Atkinson and Moon, 1994). City Challenge was in the process of being developed during the most recent period of urban unrest in the early 1990s. The bidding guidance for City Challenge highlighted crime as among the Government's key aims for the competition, but did not signal enhancing youth opportunities or addressing youth disadvantage as key components of the programme.

The ground rules changed with the launch of SRB and a youth focus was stimulated by the bidding guidance. This states that Challenge Fund schemes might aim to:

> ... enhance the employment prospects, education and skills of local people, particularly the young and those at a disadvantage.

SRB supports a more diverse range of approaches to regeneration than City Challenge and the Scottish Urban Partnerships, which focused solely on comprehensive, area-based regeneration. Consequently, it has facilitated the development of schemes around specific 'themes' or priority groups, including young people. A number of successful bids focused entirely on youth were funded in the second and third rounds of SRB, suggesting the coming of age of a specific youth focus within urban regeneration initiatives. This has continued with the announcement of the successful SRB4 bids in 1998, around 30% of which are solely focused on youth.

Thus, the spotlighting of young people as an issue for concern in urban regeneration does not have a long history, although the problems caused by, rather than confronted by, young people have been prominent for longer. The emphasis on 'problem youth' has continued under the present Government, particularly in relation to the Crime and Disorder Bill. However, it does appear to have a more rounded youth agenda, with the emphasis also on creating work and training opportunities for young people through the New Deal, as well as improving educational achievement.

## Community participation and young people

It is now firmly accepted that sustainable regeneration requires the active participation of local communities. It is also recognised that residential communities contain diverse groups with distinctive needs. Even in the poorest areas, some groups, such as young people, people with disabilities or minority ethnic groups, may be more marginalised than others. As a result, power disparities may exist within communities leading to the interests of some groups being over-represented in local organisations.

Research has indicated that typical community activists tend to be older people, often pensioners, and they have usually lived in the locality for some time (Macfarlane and Mabbot, 1993). Young people are generally under-represented in local forums and community organisations (Lightfoot, 1990). However, as young people's needs and concerns have moved into the spotlight, the need to actively engage them in the process of change has become apparent. In addition, the legal and cultural shifts mentioned earlier concerning the rights of children and young people have also raised the profile of youth voice. As will be seen in Chapters 4 and 5, however, 'youth empowerment' involves a variety of agendas beyond simply ensuring that young people's voices are heard in regeneration structures.

## Aims and methods of the research

The main aim of this research was to examine how area-based regeneration initiatives had included young people in two respects:

3

- in what ways and to what extent have young people's needs been addressed by regeneration programmes and projects?

- in what ways and to what effect have young people been involved in decision making about regeneration?

The study sought to identify examples of good practice in relation to including young people in urban regeneration at strategic, programmatic and project levels.

The study involved focused case studies of regeneration initiatives from across the UK. Twelve initiatives were selected on the basis of a national trawl which involved examining published lists of regeneration schemes, and identifying those with a significant youth focus on the basis of strategy documents and discussions with officials. Those selected reflected a variety of scales and locations, and both top-down and bottom-up approaches:

- *Foothold*, Llanelli. An organisation providing business premises and advice to young people, established in 1990. Foothold is funded by European, Lottery and private sector sources.

- *Kingsmead Community Trust*, Kingsmead Estate, Hackney, London. A community-based voluntary organisation established in 1993 to organise social activities and provide a voice for residents in a deprived housing estate. A key focus is youth crime.

- *Greater Shankill Partnership*, Shankill, Belfast. A wide-ranging regeneration partnership with fairly substantial attention to projects for young people and youth involvement. The formal Partnership Board was formed in 1996, but this built on the work of an informal partnership operating since 1990.

- *Young Batley*, Batley, Yorkshire. A youth initiative which is linked to Batley City Challenge established in 1993. It includes several projects for young people and a youth forum and is regarded as a model for other regeneration schemes.

- *Newtown South Aston City Challenge*, Birmingham. A City Challenge established in 1993, with most of its activities centred on property development and housing improvement. The initiative attempted to

tackle various youth issues, including young people's participation, but without much success.

- *Moss Side Initiative*, Manchester (SRB1 and 2). A set of regeneration initiatives in a disadvantaged area of Manchester where there are a range of projects focused on young people.

- *Dingle 2000*, Liverpool (SRB1). A programme with a substantial youth focus and a developing youth voice in the regeneration process.

- *Youth to the Future*, South Tyneside (SRB2). A totally youth-focused borough-wide regeneration programme with a wide range of projects mainly aimed at youth unemployment.

- *Young People in Focus*, Sandwell, West Midlands (SRB3). A larger, solely youth-focused SRB programme with substantial attention to achieving an effective voice for young people. The initiative sits within a set of interlocking SRB projects funded within rounds 1, 2 and now 4. Youth involvement was largely inspired by the experience of Tipton Challenge in Sandwell.

- *Leeds Partnership with Young People*, Leeds (SRB3). A very substantial SRB programme covering a large area of north and west Leeds. Many projects planned, but most had yet to get off the ground at the time of the fieldwork.

- *Ferguslie Park Partnership*, Paisley. A flagship Scottish Urban Partnership established in 1989 with the aim of comprehensive regeneration of a very deprived housing estate. It has several youth-focused projects and specific mechanisms for involving young people.

- *Inverclyde Priority Partnership Area*, Inverclyde. An area-based project established in 1996 with some attention to youth issues and plans to involve young people. It covers the most deprived housing areas in the local authority area.

There were three stages of fieldwork:

- A preliminary assessment of each initiative was made through reviewing the scheme's documentation and data; face-to-face discussions with key actors; and group discussions with young people connected with the initiative in some way.

- Six of the 12 case studies were then selected for further, more intensive research on the basis that they seemed to have the most to offer in terms of lessons for other initiatives. These were Shankill, Batley, Moss Side, Dingle, Sandwell and Ferguslie Park. The range of actors interviewed at this stage was substantially extended. Also, additional group discussions were held with young people involved with the initiative, and discussions were held with young people who used local youth facilities but were unconnected to the main regeneration scheme.

- Feedback seminars were convened in each of the six second phase case studies to present the overall findings of the research, and comments from participants in these seminars informed the final draft of the report.

# Urban regeneration: responding to young people's needs?

## Views on young people's needs

All the regeneration initiatives in this study were a response, in some form, to the needs of young people. However, it was apparent that the responses varied very markedly between the initiatives, and there were strong contrasts between the views of young people on what their needs were, and those of decision makers on the needs of youth.

Table 1 is derived from the interviews with young people and with decision makers, including officials of regeneration agencies and elected council members, as well as from regeneration documents. It shows some powerful contrasts, and some important similarities.

Jobs and youth facilities appear high on both lists. However, the way that young people thought about jobs differed from decision makers. Young people were directly interested in obtaining jobs or better jobs, while decision

makers, perhaps more realistically, were concerned with increasing the employability of young people, for example, through training and education. Young people evinced little interest in training, and less in education, often reflecting their own previously negative experiences.

The undisputed number one priority for young people in every case study was for more leisure facilities, reflecting the perennial complaint "there's nothing to do around here". For example, in Newtown South Aston it was reported:

> "In terms of things to do, nothing, unless you've got a steady income. You find things to do like bowling or you go to the cinema, things like that, ... for those that have the money. But due to lack of work, that's why you tend to find a lot of people just hanging around...."

Table 1: The 'top five' needs for young people in priority order

| What decision makers want for young people | What young people want |
|---|---|
| 1 Jobs, training, qualifications<br>2 Developed capacities/self-esteem<br>3 Alternatives to anti-social and criminal behaviour<br>4 Improved youth facilities<br>5 Youth involvement in the regeneration process | 1 Affordable, accessible and appropriate leisure facilities<br>2 Job opportunities<br>3 To stop police harassment<br>4 To gain adult respect<br>5 To change outsiders' perceptions of them and where they live |

*Source: Interviews and documentary sources*

Similarly, in Sandwell:

> "Basically, there's nothing to do in this area. There are two night-clubs and that's it, and the only reason to visit the night-clubs is to fight. There are quite a lot of pubs, one on every corner … apart from that it's pretty dull and boring, nothing to do."

Leisure was central to the quality of life of young people, as a key source of friendship networks and self-identity, particularly in the absence of work, full-time education or family responsibilities. While some young people were vague about their needs, others had specific criticisms of what was available locally and had concrete suggestions. Commercially-provided leisure was too expensive, but this problem also arose with public provision, such as sports centres. There were also significant criticisms of youth clubs: they were not open at weekends, and held little interest for young women. The accessibility of existing facilities was also a problem – many were said to be too far away or expensive to reach.

Many decision makers also recognised youth facilities as a priority but not to the same degree. There was also a tendency to link youth facilities to the resolution of other problems, notably diverting young people from 'hanging around on street corners', and promoting youth participation in the planning or management of facilities.

Young people identified priorities which did not figure at all among the older adults. Most prominent among these was police harassment which impacted on young people in every case study area, albeit with varying levels of severity. The most difficult circumstances were apparent in the bigger cities, but it was a serious issue everywhere, both for young men and women, and for all ethnic groups, although young black men suffered most acutely. In Moss Side young people commented that they had to allow an extra 15 minutes to go anywhere in case they were stopped by police. In Sandwell, a youth forum member complained about being moved on:

> "The police should remember it's our streets – not the police's streets."

There were also broader demands for more respect and less discrimination. While participation in the labour market or in training schemes, and occasionally involvement in regeneration initiatives, were possible routes to achieving more respect, young people also stressed the need for adults to adopt less negative attitudes towards them. In addition, young people felt discriminated against in the wider world because of the stigma attached to the deprived neighbourhoods which they came from, and this was believed to influence their work and educational opportunities.

Decision makers perceived a number of needs among young people relating to participation and empowerment, although this perception was not much shared by young people. These needs related to ideas about good governance and the sustainability of regeneration initiatives, but also to developing young people's confidence and attitudes, and training them as future community leaders. Youth involvement in regeneration initiatives had largely been promoted by professionals and politicians rather than community activists. Their motivations for doing so are explored in Chapter 4.

## The urban regeneration response

Urban regeneration initiatives tend to have multiple objectives concerned with economic and social development, and physical improvement, together intended to turn around the fortunes of a deprived area. The initiatives considered here are distinctive in that objectives concerned with young people figured prominently in almost all of them, either at the overall level of the regeneration initiative, or in the shape of a specific youth strategy. Where this was not the case, attention to young people was paid through more general objectives, such as education or empowerment.

The objectives, projects and programmes regarding youth in the 12 case studies fell into five main categories.

*Economic development and employment*

Economic development objectives specific to youth were invariably tied back to young people's poor performance in the labour market. A few of the schemes had a predominately economic orientation; for example, South Tyneside, which has consistently had the second or third highest unemployment level in Great Britain, put nearly all its emphasis on jobs and preparing for jobs. Foothold, particularly, had only economic objectives. However, most schemes contained economic development objectives alongside a wide range of others.

The weight of projects in pursuit of economic development objectives concentrated on improving young people's skills and orientation to work (ie, increasing the supply of quality labour), or on connecting young people in the target area with the job opportunities that already existed, thereby assisting take-up of jobs. Relatively few projects were directly concerned with new job creation (the main concern of young people). The most notable exception was Foothold, where the whole initiative was designed to support young people's businesses. It has supported the formation of over 250 businesses, providing some 400 jobs, in eight years.

Within more broadly-based regeneration initiatives there were also projects aimed at increasing business start-ups and expanding the number of jobs available to young people. For example, at South Tyneside one project was designed to channel able young people into self-employment, and another was aimed at encouraging new business starts generally, but also had targeted financial support to assist new firms to train and employ young people. Other examples which helped to directly create opportunities for young people were sponsored apprenticeship schemes at Ferguslie Park and Batley.

Most of the effort towards achieving economic objectives, however, went on supply-side projects designed to improve employability and provide work experience. Some of these projects were expansions of mainstream initiatives, such as training for NVQs, or local examples of well-known schemes such as Groundwork. Many were designed to produce accreditation which could be used as a lever to obtain formal training or employment. But it was recognised in a number of case studies that many young people were completely disconnected with the world of work, and

special outreach measures were required. For example, at South Tyneside, detached youth work was expanded under SRB with the aim of contacting young people in the streets and encouraging their participation in education, sport and leisure, thereby increasing their self-esteem. At Dingle, targeted outreach work was undertaken by the local jobs and training agency, Dingle Opportunities, to connect disaffected young people with job and training opportunities. The Skills Challenge project at Moss Side was involved in a similar process.

Another set of innovative projects found across a number of case studies were designed to increase young people's self-confidence and improve their skills through sport, arts and culture. Examples included training in visual and performing arts at South Tyneside linked to an existing Arts Centre, a music production project at Newtown South Aston, the opportunity to gain qualifications in sports coaching at Moss Side, and opportunities to train as a DJ in Ferguslie Park. These kinds of projects were highly attractive to young people, and had the advantage of developing transferable as well as specialist skills.

Altogether, these kinds of projects were central both to the regeneration agenda and to the concerns that young people have about the lack of jobs. It was not possible within the confines of this study, however, to comment on their impact. What did seem clear was that economic objectives are being pursued with vigour, young people's needs have clearly been put on the agenda, and that the youth focus has helped to encourage a number of exciting and innovative projects which are successfully engaging young people, even those who have become highly disconnected from the labour market.

### Education

Many of the case studies had the aim of increasing the level of educational attainment and preventing disadvantaged young people dropping out of education entirely. Education assumed an especially high priority in the cases of Sandwell, whose performance as a local authority in the school league tables was particularly poor; Shankill with its acknowledged cultural bias against good educational performance; and Ferguslie where education had been 'discovered' as an issue during the period of the initiative.

Education projects usually reached well down the age range, often to primary schools and even below, and sometimes extended to parents, in recognition that parental attitude is a major factor in educational development. The most significant example of this was the Early Years project at Shankill, which aimed to give children and their parents support from the moment they are born. The idea was to raise self-confidence and esteem and 'open up pathways of opportunity'. Many other projects developed as components of regeneration initiatives aimed to support school children, such as the Young Families Education Initiative at South Tyneside, and the STEPs project at Sandwell, which aimed to track the progress of individual schoolchildren. Projects focused on older groups included literacy projects and careers guidance for disaffected pupils.

Some education projects employed 'peer educators' in order to provide role models for discouraged or disaffected young people. At Shankill, some of the workers on the Early Years project were themselves young parents.

Information Shops targeted at young people were a feature of some initiatives. These were typically located in town centres and aimed to provide information about topics such as jobs, training, education, health, drugs and housing. However, these projects seemed to be too unfocused to be of genuine value to enquirers, and were not well used. At South Tyneside they were also used as the base for outreach youth workers, and it seemed possible that their value might be greater as a result. At Batley the Information Shop had found a role as a centre for developing information technology (IT) skills.

A notable omission was much attention to increasing access to further and higher education. While there were some projects which aimed to provide advice, for example, at Moss Side, to a large extent the educational needs of those over 16 were left aside. Efforts were largely concentrated on training and employment, and there seemed to be little expectation that underachievement at school could be compensated for afterwards.

It is clear that the attention given to education in regeneration agendas was consistent with one of the key disadvantages faced by young people and with the need to enhance local knowledge and skills levels in pursuit of economic development. However, education was not an issue which young people themselves prioritised, probably because of their often poor experience of the education system as children.

### Quality of life

'Quality of life' embraces a wide range of projects concerned with everyday, lived experience. All of the broadly-focused regeneration initiatives included some quality of life objectives, including housing, crime, health and local facilities, which were designed to address the social objectives of regeneration by combating the effects of deprivation.

However, direct attention to young people's quality of life was rare. Probably the only major example was at Leeds whose SRB bid prominently recognised poor housing and environment, lack of facilities and 'health, drugs and crime' as three of six key problems to be addressed. The latter two seemed to have come into scope because of consultation with young people. The Leeds project was also significant because it firmly recognised "something to do and somewhere to go" as a legitimate aspiration which required a response.

In the majority of cases, quality of life was a secondary consideration and usually emerged out of other objectives. For example, sports and arts projects provided 'something to do' but were largely driven by concerns over improving young people's skills and orientation towards work. Leisure activities, for example, at Moss Side, were provided because they were 'diversionary' and aimed at young people at risk of offending. Even the housing project at South Tyneside was designed primarily to help break the 'no home/no job' spiral.

Shankill and Moss Side both planned to build large youth centres, with meeting spaces, cafes, facilities for concerts and dance events, arts studios, internet access and sport and recreation space. While these facilities were welcomed by young people, the benefits were not always clear and there was some suspicion that they were driven by funding opportunity rather than by a clear assessment of needs. Hardly any consideration had been given in any regeneration initiative to the development of smaller-scale youth facilities.

Police harassment was considered by young people to be a major problem which affected their quality of life. However, there were no substantial projects in any area which attempted to tackle this, although at Moss Side the local 'community safety' project produced credit-card size leaflets which provided advice to young people on what to do if stopped by police. This was later imitated at Newtown South Aston. Both of these initiatives were regarded locally as highly contentious.

Overall, then, urban regenerative initiatives did more directly to improve young people's quality of life than their objectives suggested, but this was a spin-off in most cases from concerns with improving young people's economic position. Many of the projects were small scale and poorly funded, although there were notable exceptions. Some significant problems which young people said they faced in daily life remained off the agenda in most cases.

### Social control

While no regeneration initiative had been devised explicitly to control 'problem youth', a handful of initiatives regarded the social control of young people as important enough to feature as part of a published strategy. For example, in Batley, a specific 'operational objective' is:

> ... to control crime and anti-social behaviour among the current generation of young people.

Similarly in Moss Side, 'disaffected young people' were seen as the main target groups of youth-related projects.

A number of initiatives included diversionary projects; for example, a rash of car and motorcycle projects designed in the wake of 'joyriding'. Social control projects were a response to funding opportunities presented by the former Government, especially under City Challenge, or a perception of its agenda. Regeneration officials did not generally share this perspective and, as regeneration projects

matured, there was decreasing attention to this aspect.

On the whole, apart from the fear of victimisation felt by many young people outside their own territories, young people themselves did not express their needs in terms that could be addressed by social control objectives or projects. On the contrary, what many of them wanted was to be treated with more respect, and not to be classified as a problem just because they were young.

### Empowerment

Empowering and involving young people is the final category of objectives and projects. This was an objective of all but one of the 12 initiatives. The range of projects under this heading is considered in the next chapter.

## Urban regeneration strategies

The degree of success with which regeneration initiatives respond to needs depends not only on the range of objectives and projects, but also on the broader strategies which are followed in order to reach these objectives. There were three key elements of strategy among the case studies related to their orientation towards young people.

### Resources

The resources devoted to projects for young people in most cases seemed minimal compared to the overall size of the project, and the number of young people in the area.

There were a number of difficulties in pinning down the level of resources devoted to youth projects in this study. In the case of the solely youth-focused initiatives the answer was fairly clear, but in the majority of cases, where there was a wide-ranging regeneration initiative with some identifiable youth projects, it was very hard to disaggregate fully the youth dimension.

Batley City Challenge and the youth-focused SRB3 initiatives at Sandwell and Leeds were the best funded schemes. Considered in terms of spending per young person in the target population, Batley's budget translated into £38 per young person per year, Sandwell's £43 and Leed's £510. All the others were tiny in comparison to these.

Inevitably, relatively small numbers of young people were benefiting in comparison to the size of the target populations, even in the large projects.

## Targeting

The youth elements of the regeneration strategies were targeted along two main dimensions: the age of young people, and types of young people. A third, less important, dimension was to target young people in particular areas, as at Sandwell.

*Targeting by age.* In this study 'young people' were considered to be those aged between 16 and 24. However, although there were a few active participants at or beyond the upper end of this age range, in reality the focus of attention in most projects and programmes was on a younger age group, aged 14-19. A few initiatives also targeted younger school students, such as educational support projects in Sandwell, Leeds and North Tyneside.

There were two main reasons for the 14-19 focus. First, there was felt to be an important opportunity to alter personal trajectories in the transitional period between youth and adulthood. Second, young people in this age range seemed to form a common interest group, and could be easily organised. The narrow and relatively young age range catered for by regeneration initiatives has important implications for the processes of youth involvement, considered later in the report.

Across the initiatives there was little attention to the particular needs of people in their 20s. Where projects did cater for this group it was usually incidental. For example, Foothold supported several young entrepreneurs in their 20s and a project in Moss Side, also focusing on young businesses, had an older client group. In some cases, the absence of focus on people in their 20s was explained as deriving from a sense that those with problems in this age group were a 'lost cause' and not, therefore, amenable to reform. There was one exception to this pattern, however. In Kingsmead, young men in their 20s were seen as the most problematic

group on the estate and projects were therefore devised specifically for them.

*Types of young people.* There were three broad approaches to targeting types of young people. The first was to mainly target 'disaffected' young people. Disaffection was defined in different ways, but the symptoms were often said to be criminality, vandalism, drug misuse and dropping out of school – in other words, young people who were alienated from adult values or adult institutions. In Kingsmead, the behaviour of young men was the prime reason for the development of the community trust which was at the centre of regeneration action. At Moss Side, targeting disaffected youth was clearly a product of the social control element of the main regeneration objectives. In Sandwell, also, where the main emphasis was not on disaffection, there was still a concern about 'the missing 10%', disappeared from the records and assumed to be socially disconnected. The targeting of 'disaffection' tended to imply that young men, rather than women, were the problem.

In some cases it was evident that 'disaffected' young people were believed to be a threat to the success of the regeneration initiative. This was particularly the case at Newtown South Aston where it was reported by a community development officer that the city council had put to the Government the rationale that:

> "... unless we tackle the issue of disaffection then we may be undermining the whole programme."

Generally, disaffection was seen as having its roots in disadvantage, and all projects which targeted disaffected youth targeted disadvantage too. In several case studies the links between disaffection and disadvantage were made explicitly. At Moss Side, for example, it was believed:

> "... [young people] are at particular risk. Often without jobs or appropriate training they can see the bad role models of drug dealers in everyday close contact."

Disadvantaged young people were targeted by all case studies. A priority group which was mentioned frequently was ethnic minorities whom, statistics showed, were particularly disadvantaged. Sometimes it was implied that every young person living in the target area was a potential beneficiary of the initiative, therefore the possibility was left open that the actual beneficiaries of programmes might not be the most disadvantaged.

A third approach, in South Tyneside and Sandwell only, was to target better educated groups of young people. The aim was, in part, to retain more graduates, college leavers and those with 'A'-levels in the local job market. This translated into the 'Retaining Success' project at North Tyneside and the 'High Achievers' project at Sandwell.

### Synthesis/coordination

There was only evidence in a few case studies that the youth-related projects which took place within regeneration initiatives were logically programmed and well integrated with each other, and with existing youth provision.

The worst problems with coordination were at Shankill and Moss Side. While the Greater Shankill Partnership was a self-contained regeneration initiative with a strategy for its area and its own management board and small staff, it was clear that there was a vast array of other projects focused on youth (and on regeneration) which were not part of the Partnership's programme. There were two reasons for this. First, the very large amounts of money from different sources available in Northern Ireland for regeneration purposes and for encouraging political calm. These include European Union (EU) Structural Funds, the Peace and Reconciliation Fund, and the International Fund for Ireland, as well as funding through Making Belfast Work, the Government's regeneration agency. Second, although Shankill is a solely Protestant/Unionist area there are divisions by neighbourhood, church, political and paramilitary loyalties. The approach seemed to be that in an area with such deep-seated problems any kind of project was worthwhile. Moreover, if there was a project in a sub-area dominated by one grouping, other areas would also demand (and get) a similar project.

The difficulties in Moss Side seemed to result from initiatives which overlapped in space and time. Competitive regeneration funding through City Challenge in neighbouring Hulme was followed by SRB funding in rounds 1 and 2. There then came an EU-funded URBAN programme which is now underway. However, prior to any of these, the area had already been a priority for the city council and there was a large number of continuing projects. The 'Moss Side Initiative' included all of these elements. However, the reality was a wide range of projects, continually repackaged in line with new funding opportunities and developments, which few staff seemed to understand, except a handful in the council's chief executive's department.

On the other hand, some initiatives had a sense of an overall vision, a coherent set of objectives, a logical fit between projects and objectives, and a timetable. The best examples were at South Tyneside and Sandwell. At the former, the predominately economic-focused initiative was conceived as a series of steps starting with raising educational achievement and ending with creating jobs. There was also a deliberate attempt to fill gaps in mainstream provision. At Sandwell, SRB3 was integrated with other regeneration initiatives in space and time, and was subject to a common management process. The initiative was also linked to the policy development process in the council's youth service. The 'Young People in Focus' initiative itself had a carefully designed and well-integrated set of projects, and there was provision within it to develop further projects, especially those identified by young people, using uncommitted SRB money.

Most of the initiatives stood between these extremes – the projects were reasonable responses to the problems with a clear role in regeneration, but it was hard to see that the projects added to more than the sum of their parts. There seem to be two main reasons for this. First, the overall level of resources was very small in relation to the needs. Where this was the case it inevitably meant that the initiative was scratching at the surface of the problems and it was hard to be strategic. Second, there was a tendency for youth projects to be compartmentalised and isolated from the mainstream. While it may be a strength to 'put youth on the agenda' (it ensures young people are not forgotten), there was also a danger that youth issues were thought to have been taken care of.

## Conclusions

Young people's views about their own needs differed in important ways from the perspectives on the needs of youth held by regeneration officials, politicians and community representatives. Largely, regeneration objectives and projects were dominated by adults' perspectives. This means that 'somewhere to go' was de-emphasised, the need for respect was approached only indirectly, the issue of police harassment almost ignored, and education given more emphasis than young people would give it. To some extent the differences may be explained by the definition of the regeneration agenda in response to government initiatives, but there were also genuine intergenerational differences in the perspectives of what is important. The discrepancy in views between adults and young people revealed in this research lends weight to the arguments for youth 'voice' projects discussed in the next chapter.

Overall, though, the approach of regeneration initiatives was largely encouraging: it seems clear that they are starting to take on board many of the important needs of young people. Although the regeneration agenda is not so much concerned with quality of life issues as it used to be, the switch away from housing and property-led approaches to regeneration towards more emphasis on skills and education in pursuit of economic development has favoured a focus on youth.

It was not possible to evaluate individual projects within the confines of this research, but some general strategic points can be made. While the overall resources devoted to projects for young people were very low in most cases, it seems likely that disadvantaged and disaffected young people will feature prominently among the beneficiaries. It is a cause for concern, however, that young people in their 20s are often considered 'a lost cause' and are largely ignored. Clearly, better coordination of youth projects within initiatives would enhance the impact of regeneration funds, and the 'compartmentalising' of youth within regeneration is a particularly difficult strategic issue.

# Involving young people: mechanisms and structures

## Mechanisms for youth involvement

There was a wide range of mechanisms for involving young people employed in the case studies. These are summarised in Table 2, together with their advantages and disadvantages, and reviewed in the following discussion according to the level of youth participation involved.

Youth forums were by the far the most popular mechanism of participation. These are discussed later in the chapter as they cut across all of these levels and types of participation.

### Consultation

Youth surveys were structured questionnaires used to investigate the lifestyle, attitudes and needs of young people. They were useful in ascertaining the views of a large and representative group but, like all surveys, they collected fairly superficial information, and only offered young people a minimal input into decision making, with no scope for capacity-building or personal interaction. Youth surveys were, therefore, often followed up with more intensive methods of participation. Some surveys attempted to meet development objectives as well as collect information. For example, a 'youth audit' conducted in Moss Side by researchers at Manchester Metropolitan University attempted to be more process-orientated than most surveys by involving young people in defining the research focus. Other surveys used young people themselves as interviewers after appropriate training, for example, at Sandwell.

The second consultation technique we encountered was youth conferences. These were typically one-day events which involved 40-80 young people. The format adopted usually was to spend most of the day in workshop sessions discussing issues affecting young people, with panel discussions involving decision makers such as councillors taking place at the end of the day.

Youth conferences had a number of advantages as a means of involving young people:

- they involved personal interaction and mutual learning between young people and adults;

- they were capacity-building as well as consultative exercises as young people were usually involved in planning the conference and facilitating workshops;

- they can have some political impact as commitments undertaken at a public conference are difficult to ignore.

Youth conferences inspired enthusiasm from all involved, and often provided the momentum for longer-term strategies for youth participation.

The main disadvantage of youth conferences was that generally only 'bussable' young people attended, that is, those who were already linked to youth organisations such as schools, youth clubs and uniformed organisations. 'Unclubbable' and older young people were unlikely to be involved.

Focus groups were employed in some case studies. They never reached large numbers of young people, but it was evident that a rolling programme of interviews with different sets of young people could generate good quality information from a sample which is not self-selecting. This method also reached 'unclubbable youth' using detached youth work methods to meet young people on their 'territory'. While focus groups also involved personal interaction between officials and young people, they did not involve any

**Table 2: Mechanisms for youth involvement**

| Method of involvement | Level of participation | Advantages | Disadvantages |
|---|---|---|---|
| Youth surveys | Consultation | • Large numbers of young people involved | • Superficial information<br>• Minimal level of involvement<br>• No capacity-building or personal interaction |
| Youth conferences | Consultation | • Personal interaction and mutual learning<br>• Capacity-building<br>• Political impact | • Only young people linked to youth groups involved |
| Focus groups | Consultation | • Broad range of young people can be involved, including disaffected<br>• Meeting young people on their territory<br>• Potential for personal interaction | • No capacity-building<br>• Limited level of involvement |
| Management of projects | Joint management | • Promotes youth 'ownership' of projects | • Small number of (selected) young people involved<br>• Danger of tokenism<br>• Narrow focus of involvement |
| Youth delegates on partnership boards and community forums | Joint management | • Potential for wide-ranging involvement<br>• Can be close to the 'real power'<br>• Capacity-building and personal interaction | • Danger of tokenism<br>• Small number of (selected) young people involved<br>• Most young people prefer parallel structures |
| Delegated power | Control | • Potential to have significant impacts<br>• Capacity-building | • Generally small scale and narrowly focused involvement<br>• Small number of (selected) young people involved |
| Youth-owned projects | Control | • Reflects young people's interests and priorities | • Narrow focus of involvement<br>• Relies on imaginative and enthusiastic young people taking the initiative |

significant capacity-building for young people unless peer researchers were used.

## Joint management

There were two forms of joint management. The first type was youth representation on the management boards of specific projects, such as youth or media centres. This type of involvement had the advantage of making projects appear 'youth-owned'. However, it was difficult to gauge the influence which youth delegates had on these boards in practice. Also, involvement tended to have a narrow focus, usually on leisure facilities rather than on projects more central to the regeneration agenda, such as education and training.

The second, and more common, type of joint management was having youth delegates on partnership boards and community forums. Young people had representatives at board level in four case studies and, in a further two cases, Batley and Ferguslie Park, there were youth delegates on the community forum who had access to the board. Young people who are members of a partnership board had the potential to be close to the centre of power. However, the very formal, and often political, nature of board meetings often made it a difficult environment for a young person to make a contribution. Also, partnership boards were often 'rubber-stamping' bodies, and therefore not the most appropriate level for young people to make an impact. There was only one case, Sandwell, where young people were represented on the sub-committees of the partnership where decisions were effectively made. Some youth delegates found community forum meetings a more welcoming environment than partnership boards. However, these were generally large gatherings which young people found very boring and consequently their attendance was often poor. In any case, it appeared that young people's influence could be diluted if channelled through a community forum dominated by adults.

In all of these forms of joint management there was clearly a danger of tokenism because young people usually had a minority representation on a committee dominated by adults. This was acknowledged by one senior officer:

> "It is just symbolism. So it is good that there are two people representing the cause of youth on the Management Group, even if one doesn't say anything and one doesn't get on with politicians, but never mind."

Also, participation on these boards involved only a small number of young people, and often they were selected or self-selected rather than elected representatives. Very few young people relished being the only youth representative in a large group of adults, preferring instead to be involved in parallel youth structures. However, in several case studies there was an exceptional young person who seemed able to take on that role and make some kind of impact.

## Control

Elements of 'control' exist where young people have been given delegated power over projects, or where a project has been conceived and run by young people themselves.

Delegated power tended to be given only over small-scale projects. For example, in Batley the Youth Forum had control over the Youth Resource Bank, a fund to purchase pieces of equipment; they decided to spend all of it on a minibus. The Sandwell Youth Forum enjoyed the most substantial delegated power among our case studies. It had been given control of the 'Pilot Projects Development Fund', a challenge fund for local youth groups which had a total budget of £350,000 over seven years.

Projects which are defined as 'youth-owned' are those which young people have developed on their own initiative, secured funding for and managed. Among all 12 case studies there was only one example.

Made Safe in Dingle was the only example of an entirely youth-owned, bottom-up project in the study. Its activities centre around music and visual arts. It involves a core group of around 15 young people under the age of 30, and there are another 30 young people associated with it in some way.

This project was initiated by two young men who perceived a lack of facilities for young people to develop and use their artistic skills in Dingle. Its aims are to develop a community business to facilitate local people wishing to initiate arts activities in Dingle; to organise exchanges and other visits which will allow Dingle people to learn from activities taking place elsewhere; and to help local people find jobs in arts and cultural activities. This initiative has been supported by a range of other projects associated with the Dingle 2000 SRB, and has received funding from a number of sources, including the SRB Community Chest. Made Safe was perceived very positively by our interviewees in Dingle as helping to show what young people can do for themselves.

## Youth forums

Youth forums and councils are not a new concept. The Northern Ireland Youth Forum, for example, was established in 1979. However, they have recently been given a significant boost by the increased emphasis on youth 'voice' in urban regeneration initiatives and within local Government following reorganisation. Youth forums were by far the most popular instrument for encouraging youth involvement in urban regeneration. Nine of the 12 case studies either had a youth forum or planned to develop one.

### Types and constitution of youth forums

Youth forums can be defined as a structure for youth involvement which is separate from, and usually parallel to, adult representative structures. The longest established youth forum among the case studies, Young Batley, had been running for over four years. The others had all been in existence for considerably shorter periods. All had been developed in consequence of the regeneration initiative in their area, and most received the bulk of their funding from the initiative.

The seven forums which were operational at some point during our research can be categorised as follows:

- Sandwell and Batley youth forums were formal and high profile structures in receipt of relatively generous funding and considered to be a constituent part of the regeneration initiative;

- Ferguslie Park, Shankill and Dingle were less formal organisations with lower levels of resources, but were linked in some way to the structures of the regeneration initiative;

- Newtown South Aston had an active youth forum serving young people from the Bangladeshi community only; it received some practical and financial support, but was not connected to the structures of the regeneration initiative; it acted more as a self-help group for young people facing a common set of problems;

- Moss Side was the most informal youth forum; it was a loose grouping of young people who had met a few times, and had no independent resources and only minimal links with wider regeneration structures.

The forums related to widely differing geographical scales: the Sandwell Youth Forum covers an urban area of 300,000 people; Ferguslie Park Youth Forum is limited to a housing estate with less than 6,000 residents.

Typically, youth forums were initiated through existing youth groups nominating two representatives to attend a meeting to develop a forum. In other cases the original members of the youth forum were recruited at a youth conference or from existing youth forums. Most youth forums were dominated by those in the 14- to 19-year-old age band. Membership was usually said to be in the region of 30-80 young people, however, only a small number were ever actively involved in the activities of the youth forum (around 10-15 young people). In Young Batley there was a core, voting membership, but elsewhere all members, except office bearers, seemed to have equal status. The broader group often seemed to be members in name only, or simply attended for social events. In practice, youth forums usually took the form of loosely constituted committees of a small number of young people which experienced a high turnover of active membership.

Of the seven active youth forums, only Batley, Shankill and Ferguslie Park had written constitutions. The lack of a written constitution elsewhere was partly attributable to the desire by adults to let young people set up their own ways of working rather than impose rules. However, their absence seemed to create uncertainty about where power and responsibility lay, and contributed to the tendency for them not to be taken seriously.

## Why a youth forum?

Youth forums appeared to be adopted as the principal means of promoting young people's involvement within regeneration initiatives without much debate about their merits. Most adults simply thought that they seemed like a good idea. The demand for a youth forum never came from young people themselves. Rather, it was always suggested to them by officers such as youth workers, although in some cases young people had expressed an interest in having a voice of some kind.

Officers felt that the main benefit of this instrument for youth involvement was that it provided a visible structure which could facilitate the ongoing participation of young people in the regeneration process. Also, it was recognised that most young people, particularly the youngest age groups, prefer participation in parallel youth structures to direct involvement in adult representative organisations. Establishing a youth forum had the added advantage that it could be considered an output of the regeneration initiative for evaluation purposes.

## Activities

When youth forums were first set up their principal activity was to meet on a regular basis to discuss issues affecting young people, and it was normally intended that they would feed these views into wider local structures. However, unless young people had something concrete to talk about these meetings often petered out. Clearly momentum can be very quickly gained and lost in youth forums, and this is due in part to the lack of a sense of purpose. They contrast with most community forums which are set up to focus upon specific issues, such as housing conditions. Youth forums were often established on a generalist basis and the only criterion for involvement was membership of a broad social group. Consequently, they often lacked a set of values or objectives to bind them together.

Some youth forums either lost direction or simply ceased to exist. However, others maintained momentum by focusing their activities on specific objectives, such as generating a new leisure activity for young people. For example, in Ferguslie Park members of the youth forum had become heavily involved in a group called Unit X which was campaigning for a youth facility in their community. In most cases the youth forum had found some kind of role as an organising committee for youth events, such as conferences or discos. Only in Batley and Sandwell did youth forums appear to be engaged in activities relevant to the wider regeneration agenda. However, even in Batley the youth forum's main activities still seemed to centre around planning events such as youth exchanges, or discussing the use of resources for leisure activities.

## Democracy, openness and accountability

There was a range of problems pertaining to good governance presented by youth involvement in the case studies. It could be argued that, given the very limited impacts of youth forums so far (see Chapter 4), matters of governance are largely of no relevance. However, they are important if youth forums are ever to take on a genuinely political role.

First, there was a lack of democracy in youth forums and in youth involvement generally. Most young people involved in forums and other mechanisms were selected or self-selected rather than elected representatives. Self-selected volunteers are characteristic of community participation, but it was striking that professionals were far more comfortable with 'hand-picking' youth delegates than would ever be considered acceptable in adult forums. The importance of achieving a balance in youth forums between different sections of the young population (discussed below) provides a partial explanation.

Another problem was that youth forums were often regarded as 'elitist' and 'cliquey' rather than open organisations. There was a keen awareness of this problem among both young people and youth workers involved in forums, and in most cases they expressed what appeared to be genuine concern about the need to expand the membership. One young man commented that: "The more people that are interested, the more power you have". However, the tendency for youth forums to develop into a close-knit group of friends posed significant, if unintentional, barriers to the involvement of other young people. This problem appeared to be far more acute in youth than in adult forums because of the intensity of peer group relationships at this age, and the lack of confidence suffered by many young people, which makes it a very daunting prospect to join a new group.

Finally, none of the youth forums seemed genuinely accountable to a broader group of young people. Although in theory members of youth forums were often supposed to represent a particular youth club or school, there were no examples of these feedback mechanisms operating in practice. In fact, it was common for young people to switch allegiance and friendship networks from the youth group they initially represented to the youth forum.

## Characteristics of participants

One very positive finding was that in most cases the membership of youth forums did appear to reflect the local population of young people as regards factors such as gender, race and social background. To a large extent this was a product of the anti-discrimination ethic of youth workers.

*Gender and age mix.* Most youth forums had achieved a reasonable mix of male and female participants, although most of the youth delegates and office bearers in youth forums were male (as with adult community groups). However, youth groups in the case studies were generally dominated by teenagers. It may be that gender distinctions become more pronounced as young people start families because young women bear the brunt of childcare responsibilities. Particular efforts may be required to involve young women in their late teens and early 20s, especially young mothers. However, the research does not provide insight into this problem because all the

forums encountered involved younger people in significant majority.

*Race.* In all case study initiatives located in multi-racial areas youth workers had made considerable efforts to counter racism and integrate young people from different ethnic backgrounds. The youth forum in Young Batley was a conspicuous success in this regard.

There were difficult issues faced by youth workers in a number of case studies regarding the involvement of young Moslems after puberty, particularly women, because of cultural restrictions. For example, it was often not permitted for them to participate in mixed sex groups or to attend meetings which ran late into the evening. Thus structures and processes for involvement had to be developed which were sensitive to these cultural concerns.

*Disaffection.* Considerable efforts had been made in several case studies to involve disaffected or alienated young people, and these appear to have been met with some success. Youth involvement initiatives were by no means dominated by 'safe' young people. In Sandwell, for example, those setting up the youth forum resisted the offer by a head teacher of two 'prefect-type' young people as representatives to the youth forum, and opted instead to involve two young people experiencing difficulties at school. On the whole, however, the most disaffected young people did not get involved. As one officer conceded: "those who are hanging around street corners will never represent the youth of Sandwell".

*Coolness.* Another youth-specific issue to arise was that of 'coolness'. Youth workers repeatedly highlighted the importance of attracting 'cool kids' (that is, those who enjoy peer group respect) into projects in order to give them credibility with other young people. One youth worker recommended targeting the leaders of groups of young people "and the others will follow for fear of missing out". This emphasis on 'cool' kids was one reason why initiatives were not dominated by 'safe' young people.

## Links with wider regeneration structures

Most youth forums were not well linked into wider regeneration structures in their area. In

Moss Side, for example, the youth forum appeared to have been set up completely in isolation from the local regeneration and representative structures, although some steps were later taken to remedy this. More commonly, however, some provision had been made for youth representation on the partnership board and/or community forum, but these links were not proving effective in practice. For example, in Batley, the attendance of the youth forum representatives at community forum meetings was "atrocious" because they found them boring. In Shankill the youth forum had a delegate on the partnership board and three representatives on the community forum. However, the youth representatives' attendance at community forum meetings was patchy. While the youth delegate's attendance at the partnership board was acknowledged to be good, he did not attend youth forum meetings.

The Sandwell Youth Forum was the most securely linked into wider regeneration structures. It had youth delegates throughout the partnership decision-making structure up to and including the partnership board, and was an integral part of the project appraisal system for SRB3. The forum's members were also in close contact with senior regeneration staff through a mentoring programme.

### Potential disbenefits

A word of caution is required about youth forums given their current, and growing, popularity. Experience of some of the case studies suggest that there are at least three potential dangers.

First, they can be used as "the token 10 young people" to legitimise the decision making of adults, and thus provide agencies with an alternative to the meaningful participation of a broad group of young people.

Second, the members of a high profile youth forum may receive a highly disproportionate share of youth work resources in their area, such as funding for residentials and foreign trips. This is especially serious if the young people involved are not the most disadvantaged in the community. There is clearly a case for targeting youth work resources in order to maximise their effectiveness, but the existence of a youth forum may lead to excessive concentration.

Third, youth forums can actually *disempower* young people in an area if they only represent a certain section of the young population, for example, those from a particular neighbourhood. This is because participants can use their influence to skew resources towards their 'type' of young people and away from other 'types' of young people. This is only a minor concern given the limited impacts of young people's participation.

### The way forward?

Youth forums are, in many cases, experiments and some of their problems are attributable to this. The case studies show a number of factors which have helped youth forums succeed as a mechanism to represent youth:

- a clear agenda and specific set of objectives;

- opportunities for participants to have fun as well as to attend meetings, for example, leisure activities were often a useful 'hook' to draw young people into participatory mechanisms;

- arrangements for young people to regularly feed their views into the local regeneration initiative;

- being well-resourced and supported.

There is, however, a concern that they will become the only route in some areas for young people's views to be fed into the regeneration process.

The youth forum which appears to be working most effectively among our case studies is in Sandwell. There are a set of active youth forums which feed into a central Sandwell Youth Forum which is relatively well-attended and whose members take part in a range of the Regeneration Partnership's activities. Also, it appears to be having an impact upon the decisions taken by the initiative, at least at the margins. This success seems attributable to a number of factors:

- youth involvement is taken seriously at a high level;

- generous funding and a good quality of staffing;

- a reasonable period of development through the local youth forums;

- skilled and experienced staff support;

- the high calibre of the core youth activists.

Young Batley was a forerunner in youth involvement in urban regeneration and has been a high profile element of Batley City Challenge. However, it has encountered various difficulties recently. The youth forum is perceived as an insular and closed organisation, dominated by users of particular leisure projects rather than representative of all local young people. Also, while the youth forum has had some operational influence on youth-related projects, it seems to have made little contribution to wider regeneration decision making.

The problems within Young Batley seem to stem from:

- its relative isolation from other elements of City Challenge;

- a loss of momentum as City Challenge winds up;

- an excessive emphasis on the national profile of Young Batley, coupled with insufficient local outreach work to develop a sense of local ownership.

However, the lessons of Young Batley have been fed into the development of youth involvement in later SRB initiatives, and have given Kirklees Council the confidence to promote youth participation in mainstream services.

A key point to emerge was that youth forums appeared to be more appropriate for younger age groups, who were very keen on parallel youth structures, than for older young people. Young people in their late teens and 20s were reported not to want to be involved in, and were not targeted by, 'youth' groups, neither were they involved in adult community structures. It therefore seems that mechanisms for youth involvement need to be differentiated by age. This is to be expected given that 16- and 24-year-olds are at completely different stages in their transition to adulthood. The Community Learning Project in Dingle offered an approach to participation which may be particularly appropriate for the older age group as young people become equipped to become involved in a wide range of community organisations rather than forming a 'youth' group. This approach had the important advantage of bringing young people and adults together to address their concerns rather than corralling young people into a separate category.

The Community Learning Project (CLP) in Dingle is funded by SRB and the Open University. It is a community capacity-building project which uses a resource pack called *Build on Your Skills* and residential weekends to help local people to develop confidence around their own capacities. It is intended that graduates of the programme will act as peer educators in the community and that new people will become active in the regeneration process as a consequence.

The CLP was viewed very positively in Dingle because its style and ethos seems to work particularly well with groups who are traditionally under-represented in community activity. It is targeted on the whole age range, but has attracted a considerable number of young people and it played a key role in supporting a number of local young men who have became very active in local community structures.

The CLP has brought together different groups within the community from teenagers to septuagenarians, who have been able to recognise their common values and aspirations. It seems to have been particularly effective in overcoming intergenerational barriers:

"Do you know what I found amazing about it [the residential weekend]. There was young lad sitting there, my son's mate. He really listened and understood what you were on about ... the young lads and older women mixed well."

## Conclusions

The mechanisms which have been used to secure youth involvement in regeneration rely heavily on the promotion of youth forums. The evidence of the majority of these is that their purpose has not been well thought through, they are generally poorly resourced, fail the usual tests of good governance and are disconnected from regeneration decision-making structures.

Youth forums can be a useful method of involving young people if efforts are taken to resolve these problems, as the best examples show. However, it does not seem likely that they will ever represent the views of all young people, particularly older young people. They can also easily lead to young people being compartmentalised.

Including young people on partnership boards and community forums has also not been very successful as a route to involvement, as most young people tend to struggle to make a contribution.

The research suggests that there is a great deal of value in lower level forms of participation, including surveys, conferences and focus groups, which allow larger numbers to contribute and have a say. Also, there are clearly benefits in bringing adults and young people together to challenge intergenerational barriers and to jointly address the problems affecting their communities.

# Involving young people: experiences, barriers and impacts

## Adults' motivations for promoting youth involvement

Adults offered a range of rationales for promoting youth involvement in urban regeneration initiatives.

### Voice

The most common rationale for the promotion of youth participation was to give young people a voice in decision making. This was mostly a concern of regeneration officials and local councillors. There were said to be three main benefits. First, it would ensure that young people's needs would be brought to the fore. Second, it was considered that young people's needs would be met more effectively ("give them what they want") if they had been consulted. This would ensure that regeneration funds were better targeted. Third, it was said that young people would bring in "new blood" and "new ideas"; "a clarity of thought, a freshness of ideas, and an optimism which adults do not possess", according to a youth project coordinator.

### Sustainability

It was widely believed by officials that projects which had been developed with the aid of youth voice would be more sustainable because young people would feel a sense of ownership over them. It was believed that 'ownership' would translate into a higher level of use and a greater respect ("if they do it up, they'll look after it"), which has some shades of the 'problematising' attitude to youth.

### Self-development

Youth involvement was believed to help develop young people's knowledge, skills and self-esteem which would improve their life chances and hence contribute to regeneration. Although this element was not universal, there was far more emphasis on it than would be expected in relation to adults. A community activist commented:

> "If they are responsible for their own building as teenagers, then this will help them look after their families in the future."

Youth participation was also seen by some as a way of socialising problematic young people; they "might take more pride" (chair of tenants' association); they would have "nobody else to blame" and therefore "had to shape up to their responsibilities" (youth worker).

### Future citizens

Involvement of young people was also thought of as a kind of training in citizenship; they were 'future citizens' rather than present day 'fellow citizens' and they needed to be encouraged as the coming generation of community leaders. This perspective was most often voiced by community activists. One explained:

> "It's important that young people have their say; they're the citizens of tomorrow…. I'm always saying to them: 'It's us today, you tomorrow'."

## Young people's motivations for involvement

Young people became involved in participation structures for six main reasons, listed below in order of importance:

- Involvement was often simply "something to do" and a way of meeting and socialising with other young people.

- Incentives, like trips to other cities or weekend residentials, were important in sustaining the involvement of some young people, although many found that they enjoyed the stimulation of the 'work' in youth forums, such as developing bids for facilities or taking part in discussion groups.

- Changing adults' attitudes towards young people was an important motivation for many young people. One young female activist argued:

  "We have to show them that we're not all tearaways, we do know right from wrong.... I'm not slagging all adults, but some posh people 'See the state of them, they're tearaways'.... I need respect from elders for me to give them respect."

- Many young people enjoyed the opportunity to "have a voice" and "get our opinions across". Several youth delegates emphasised wanting to help to change things for the next generation of young people: "I enjoy seeing something done for the people coming up behind you, like my wee brother."

- Young people appreciated the sense of 'ownership' they derived from their involvement in specific projects like youth centres. One group of young people campaigning for a youth facility in their area explained that they wanted to be able to say: "that's ours, we fought for that."

- Some young people clearly relished the attention and responsibility they received as members of these participation structures. One ex-chair of a youth forum enthused:

  "It was brilliant. Because it was a position and everything, you had everything in your control.... [I thought] this is my opportunity to get more knowledge and organise things for other young people and make decisions and things like that.... When I was 16 and they gave me the responsibility of the keys, and the office was always open for us."

## Barriers to youth involvement

However, there was a wide range of problems and barriers in achieving involvement by young people in regeneration initiatives, some of which are also known to affect adult community activists.

### Complexity, formality and jargon

Almost all of the initiatives were complex and multifaceted and involved a wide range of partners from different sectors and organisations. The partnerships were generally managed through interlocking structures of boards and committees. Especially in SRB and other government-funded projects, intricate arrangements for planning and monitoring initiatives were part of the process. Decision making tended to be conducted in formal and jargon-ridden language and accompanied by bulky paperwork.

These difficulties also affect adult community activists, but they seemed more acute for young people. A particular barrier was the formality and length of official meetings, which young people found very off-putting. Young people also found the internal politics within partnership boards and community forums, and the long 'speeches' which adults sometimes indulged in, very tiresome.

### Nature of political power and processes

There were also difficulties regarding the dispersal of power in regeneration partnerships. The evidence of the case studies suggests the danger that young people appear to be offered power, but then find themselves with very little, as negotiation and decision making takes place behind the scenes. Some youth workers feared that the whole process of involving youth in decision making was 'setting them up to fail', as decisions were shaped by a complex power structure within which young people had little influence. Another difficulty was that young people were generally unfamiliar with the realities of political processes, or with the art of compromise.

## The attitudes and values of adults

There were some key actors in the regeneration process who openly believed that young people could not or should not be involved. Some adults felt that young people lacked the capacity for involvement. For example, a regeneration manager commented:

> "I honestly don't think young people could cope with the very ethereal and strategic level of discussion which goes on when you are trying to prepare SRB bids in line with government guidelines."

Also, some people felt that young people were downright uninterested. The chair of a tenants' association, for instance, claimed that his group had tried to get young people involved in their meetings but: "Like most youth, they don't want to know."

Some adults clearly just paid lip-service to involving young people. For example, one group of young people who made a presentation to councillors about a youth facility were angry that the councillors ignored them afterwards and took their youth worker aside to discuss the proposal. They felt that this indicated that "we were not being taken seriously". This was part of a pattern; adults in power seemed untroubled by youth workers speaking for young people, although youth workers themselves were not always comfortable with this role.

Most commonly, however, adults accepted the validity of involving young people in regeneration, but had yet to translate this into an understanding of how best to achieve meaningful involvement. In particular, most adults seemed to expect young people to adopt their language and norms of behaviour if they wished to participate, and were not prepared to listen to young people on their own terms. One councillor, for example, commented that young people often used "peer group language to abuse adults ... and terrorise older people". There was a general lack of awareness about the changes that adults may have to make in

their working practices, attitudes and behaviour to 'let young people in'. Clearly adults as well as young people require training to ensure that effective youth participation can take place.

## The attitudes and characteristics of young people

There were also barriers to youth involvement presented by the attitudes and characteristics of young people themselves, though some of these obstacles were less significant than might have been expected.

*Lack of confidence and interest in formal meetings.* Young people often had little experience of formal settings and some lacked confidence about speaking in public and dealing with 'officialdom'. There was a strong view that young people prefer 'action' to 'talking', and that this may pose difficulties where participation involves discussion or deliberation.

The process whereby young people gained confidence through participation was explained by one youth delegate who attended a community forum:

> "At the first few meetings I never used to say a word because I was the youngest person there. So when I did say something they always listened because they were shocked because I hardly said anything. I realised they wouldn't bite my head off, so that's what made me start talking more. All of them are old enough to be your dad, some of them even old enough to be your granddad. So that's why I didn't feel comfortable. But once I started saying things, I felt really comfortable because they listened."

*Territorialism.* Young people are often very territorial in their behaviour, that is, they display strong attachment to small, geographical areas such as housing estates or even parts of estates. Territorial rivalries sometimes posed significant barriers to the participation of young people from different neighbourhoods, despite the efforts of youth workers to attract young people from throughout the regeneration area.

*Cynicism and disaffection.* Cynicism and disaffection among some young people could be supposed to create serious barriers to participation. Evidence of this was mixed, however. For example, one group of young people were very cynical about the process of consultation: "we're sick of talking and nothing ever happens" and felt that politicians "could pretend they are listening." In general, however, there was far less cynicism among young people than expected. Although they were sometimes frustrated by aspects of decision making, this did not appear to cause them to lose faith in the principle of participation. Even 'uninvolved' young people did not seem dismissive of the idea of participation, and there was no evidence of young people being considered 'uncool' by their peers because they participated in initiatives.

### Time-scales and sustainability of youth groups

Building youth capacity to participate takes far longer than with adults, mainly because most youth representatives have had no prior involvement in community activism. Clearly, youth participation projects must be scheduled early in the life of an initiative if they are to make any real impact, and short-term initiatives may experience difficulties in securing any meaningful youth involvement. In Sandwell, for example, the complexity and speed of decision making within the partnership were regarded as problems for young people's participation. One senior officer conceded:

> "... we underestimated the time which would be taken to develop young people – to get them up to speed."

At the same time, there was greater pressure to make rapid progress with youth involvement because of the relatively fast turnover of participants in youth groups compared with adult groups. This was a product both of the narrowly defined age range of group membership, and the transitional nature of this phase of the lifecourse. Moving from education into work seemed to be a particularly significant transition which precipitated young people leaving youth groups, usually around the age of 18. Also, several youth workers commented that young people needed 'quick results' to sustain their interest, and had little patience for protracted political decision making. Thus the sustainability of youth groups is a significant problem.

Another time-related issue is the fact that young people are a dynamic group whose aspirations can change very quickly. The danger that youth consultation can lead to policies based on out-of-date fads had been recognised in some initiatives.

### Narrow range of interests

A frequent feature of the activities of youth forums was that they centred on generating either a new facility or a leisure activity for young people reflecting the prevailing 'nothing to do here' concerns. Many of the key projects which were central to the agenda of regeneration initiatives, for example, employment schemes, had attracted little or no youth involvement. There was evidence that young people's interests could sometimes be engaged on a broader range of issues of relevance to their age group, such as employment, education and health. For example, in Sandwell and Batley young people were involved in wide-ranging discussions over SRB4 bids. One group of young people who met with councillors in Moss Side had impressed them with the breadth of their concerns:

> "... they really wanted to talk about jobs and the perceptions of outsiders ... they actually questioned some housing issues. It was a really broad range of issues, it wasn't just very narrow."

## Support for youth involvement

### The need for additional support

The support required to secure and sustain youth involvement is significantly higher than for equivalent adult participation structures. Therefore, substantial resources are required to facilitate youth involvement and, in particular, the provision of dedicated workers emerged as crucial to effective participation. These extra support needs related largely to overcoming the barriers to youth involvement described above. Key issues were:

- young people were less experienced and confident than adults in relation to formal settings;

- youth delegates were usually 'starting from scratch' with no previous involvement in community activism;

- the high turnover of participants had significant resource implications given the intense support that young people required to become involved.

> The attempts of the youth worker in Shankill to widen the membership of the youth forum demonstrates the level of support required. She was meeting three potential new members on a weekly basis and going through the business conducted at the forum, including asking them to rehearse what they would have said had they been at the meeting. This was all preparation for them to meet with a small sub-set of the forum in two month's time with a view to them eventually joining the group.

### Training needs

Most interviewees agreed that formal training was crucial to effective youth involvement. However, most youth representatives had received very limited or no training, either because this aspect of involvement had not been fully thought through, or because insufficient resources were available.

> The voting members in Young Batley were among those to have received the most comprehensive training. The first group in 1994 received training at several residentials about constitutional matters, such as the shape of the organisation, the election of voting members, and how committees would work. Some of these young people also received training in recruitment and selection methods from the local authority. The most recent training involved developing a handbook of 'rights and responsibilities' of voting members. These include consultation, recruitment, equal opportunities and budgets.
>
> Young Batley staff have delivered most of the training and attempts to use external trainers have not been successful. According to them their approach is more appropriate because:
>
> "We emphasise you work hard and you play hard, so if you've been involved in training then you get food and there's an activity afterwards, you know, some fun."

> There are significant funds available for support and training of the Sandwell Youth Forum. One key element is a mentoring programme for members of the forum who are involved in the partnership process. Mentoring has involved senior staff, including the council's chief executive, who have regular one-to-one meetings with young people. This approach has helped to increase young people's confidence to participate as they have developed personal relationships with key players. It has also tended to reinforce the support of senior staff for youth involvement.

The experience in Batley and Sandwell suggests that the most appropriate form of training is active, problem-solving type approaches, rather than traditional classroom-based methods.

### Resources

In most areas youth involvement initiatives had been allocated very limited funds. For example, in Dingle only £7,000 funding had been set aside for launching and supporting a youth forum. Young Batley was better resourced than other youth forums, but the level of resourcing of the Sandwell Youth Forum stands in stark contrast to the other youth involvement initiatives. One third (£2.4m) of the total grant for Sandwell's SRB3 had been devoted to the objective of 'Empowering and Involving Young People'. The SRB plan indicated that £229,000 was spent on supporting the Sandwell Youth Forum and local youth forums in 1997-98, with similar amounts every year until 2004/5. Most of the money is for salaries for support workers, but funds have also been made available for residential training weekends, a high profile launch event and some fun outings. The high level of resources is a key element in the success of this youth forum.

## Impacts on regeneration projects and programmes

Young people's impact on regeneration initiatives and projects has, on the whole, been minor and limited to youth-specific issues rather than matters affecting the community as a whole. Even in Dingle where young people had a stronger voice than in most case studies, an officer commented:

"The opportunities for this age group have increased but they are not involved in shaping the direction of their area ... we don't have loads of them at meetings or involved right in the centre of what's going on."

The impact of youth involvement is not necessarily related to the structures of youth participation discussed in Chapter 3. Impact can be analysed along three dimensions. First, by the importance of issues over which control is exerted, for example, change wrought over the overall regeneration strategy through youth involvement could be considered to demonstrate more impact than change over minor project details. Second, according to whether or not established positions are changed – more impact could be assumed to exist if existing strategies to which officials are committed are altered than if new ideas are accepted. These two dimensions can be expressed in a hierarchy:

- changing a regeneration strategy (most impact);

- influencing the development of a new regeneration strategy;

- changing existing projects already established within a regeneration strategy, including operational impacts;

- influencing the development of new projects which contribute to the agreed regeneration strategy;

- influencing the development of non-strategic minor projects (least impact).

The third dimension is the degree of change which is achieved through youth participation; more impact could be assumed if changes achieved are fundamental, much less if the changes are to detail.

Table 3 shows the impacts made on regeneration initiatives by youth involvement in the case studies. In several case studies, young people were not reported to have made any impact at all on the content of the regeneration initiative. Where they did have an impact, examples of influencing or changing significant aspects of the initiatives were rare. Only in two instances did young people succeed in changing the focus at a strategic level, and both of these were in the context of planning events to which

they had been invited. At Shankill, young people themselves were instrumental in including a focus on young people as one of the regeneration initiative's strategic objectives. Their ideas "set the weekend alight" and the initiative "started taking young people's demands seriously". At Sandwell, it was young people's idea to include a project on academic 'high achievers', and the SRB3 bid was accordingly modified.

There were, however, several examples of minor contributions by young people to regeneration bids which were being developed. The focus group discussions held with young people in Leeds as the SRB3 bid was being formulated heightened the emphasis on sports and recreation in the proposal. The Kirklees SRB4 bid included a detailed project proposal for youth accommodation with built-in construction training which was based in part on ideas put forward by young people, some of them involved in Young Batley, at a residential weekend. In Sandwell an SRB4 project which involved the restructuring of a church building to create office space was modified as a result of criticisms made by the Sandwell Youth Forum.

There were few concrete examples of young people changing existing projects. First, the Sandwell Youth Forum was involved in project appraisal under SRB3 and objected to one particular project intended to develop a database to identify and tackle underachievement in Sandwell's schools. The young people felt that this was something the Council should be doing anyway and should not be funded out of the regeneration budget. As a result of young people's criticisms the project was delayed and modified. In Batley, young people's influence lead to a greatly increased emphasis on IT and computer skills at the Young Persons Information Point. Young Batley is also a key example of young people exercising operational influence over a regeneration project. The voting members were involved in the recruitment of youth work staff funded by City Challenge, and apparently also had the final say over the spending of discretionary money, such as the purchase of equipment for Young Batley activities. However, this youth influence was an informal arrangement: "It isn't actually a written thing, it's just the way we've worked." Also at Sandwell, two projects were handed over to the youth forum. Under the guidance of their support staff they ran a survey of young people and also controlled a substantial fund designed for other youth groups to develop their own projects linked to the regeneration initiative.

It was often easier for initiatives to allow young people to have influence over the development of new projects within the regeneration strategy than to change existing projects. Young people were involved in developing the plans for youth centres in Shankill (The Flagship Centre) and Moss Side (Powerhouse) by discussing the plans with the architect and making suggestions, some of which were acted upon. Although the

impact was minor, the process did seem to give young people a powerful sense of ownership over the facilities.

Some young people were involved in developing their own projects. The only example of a completely youth-owned project which also contributed to regeneration was Made Safe in Dingle. This aims to help people find jobs in arts and cultural activities and is consistent with the regeneration strategy for the area. Most of the others had no real impact on the regeneration agenda, for example concerts and dance events.

**Table 3: Impacts of youth involvement on urban regeneration initiatives**

| | Development of minor projects | Development of new projects | Changing existing projects | Influencing the development of a new strategy | Changing an existing strategy |
|---|---|---|---|---|---|
| Major influence | Dance events (Ferguslie Park and Shankill)<br><br>Youth clubs (Ferguslie Park)<br><br>Tipton Community Festival (Sandwell) | 'Made Safe in Dingle' project (Dingle) | | | |
| Moderate influence | Community radio (Ferguslie Park) | | Control over 'Somewhere To Go' and 'Pilot Projects Development Fund' (Sandwell)<br><br>Modification of Young Persons Information Point (Batley)<br><br>Involvement in staff recruitment (Batley)<br><br>Modification of STEPs educational database project (Sandwell) | | Introduction of High Achievers Project (Sandwell)<br><br>Introduced youth as a key element of the regeneration strategy (Shankill) |
| Minor influence | | Influence on detailed plans for youth centres (Shankill and Moss Side) | | Increased emphasis on sports and recreation in SRB3 (Leeds)<br><br>Involved in shaping SRB4 bids (Batley and Sandwell) | |

## Impacts on young people

A number of impacts of youth participation initiatives were apparent in relation to the individual young people involved. First, it was said everywhere that participation in initiatives such as youth forums had significantly improved the confidence, skills and knowledge of the young people involved.

Second, these young people also gained material benefits through their participation, such as opportunities for travel and taking part in leisure activities and sport, and access to IT facilities. This was particularly true of young people who were involved in the better-resourced initiatives such as Sandwell and Batley.

Third, there were numerous examples of young people's participation in these initiatives enhancing their employment prospects, both because of the skills they had gained and through personal contacts. The jobs these young people secured were mainly within the local authority's youth or leisure services rather than in the wider labour market.

Young people readily acknowledged the benefits they had gained from involvement:

> "I have been given opportunities that I wouldn't have got normally if I wasn't involved in Young Batley. You know like training courses, going places. When I wasn't involved in Young Batley I never used to travel anywhere but when I got involved in Young Batley I started travelling double the amount ... it's experience and different people to meet."

The number of young people actively involved in these initiatives was small. Therefore the positive impacts of participation were only directly experienced by a tiny proportion of the young population in any area. However, underlying this emphasis on the self-development of a limited number of young people there sometimes seemed to be the idea that they can then act as role models for other young people. There was very limited evidence on this point, but it seemed rather optimistic to think that these young people could have any significant effect on the behaviour of the bulk of their peers.

## Impacts on officials, politicians and local community representatives

It was clear from the case studies that youth involvement initiatives had a very positive impact on the way that young people were perceived by officials and councillors, particularly regarding their capacity to participate in decision making. Adults often seemed surprised by how well organised, reasonable and articulate youth delegates were. One senior manager who had been 'converted' to youth involvement commented:

> "I turned up at a meeting and these guys turned up in leather jackets, with rings through their noses, pink spiky hair. This was an evening meeting you know, after a hard day at the office, and I thought to myself 'What the bloody hell am I doing here?' And I have to say that I was totally and utterly wrong because their contribution to that meeting, it was an enlightenment to me. They were sensible, they were incisive, they had a good grasp of what the important things were, they were not frivolous, they were prepared to address serious issues. And I left the meeting a different person to when I went in."

In both Sandwell and Batley the good impression created by the youth forums had encouraged the council to promote youth involvement in mainstream services, as well as youth participation in future SRB bids. In Sandwell some officers in the youth service wanted to move towards youth management of facilities. In Batley a senior officer remarked that the youth forum had provided a "strong, positive profile for young people" and had "given the council the courage to consult young people."

Youth involvement had also significantly improved the attitude of many community activists to young people, but most interviewees were more uncertain about whether the activities of groups like youth forums had had a positive effect on the broader community. However, a senior officer at Batley believed that youth forums could facilitate community dialogue and increase older people's tolerance and understanding of young people. Also, in

Shankill it was felt that a rave run by the youth forum had helped to dispel the image of young people as destructive because it had been well organised and had caused no trouble for the local community.

## Conclusions

The experience of young people's participation in urban regeneration was that there were significant obstacles to effective participation and that the impacts of participation on the content of regeneration initiatives has been small.

The obstacles lay with both adults and young people themselves, but also with the level of support which young people's participation necessitates. Young people lacked confidence, knowledge and skills. This means that they could take a long time to develop into effective

representatives, and require quite intensive support, ideally through dedicated staff. Most adults were in favour of youth involvement but they need to be aware of the barriers which their language and working practices can create.

Youth involvement has made some difference in the approach of decision makers to young people and has reinforced positive attitudes towards youth participation. It has also been of personal benefit to individual young people, who have often significantly increased their own skills and self-confidence.

There were a few important examples of young people's participation making a difference, particularly in the examples of youth-owned projects and alteration to existing regeneration projects and strategies. However, young people's impact on regeneration initiatives was, thus far, very modest and confined to issues directly affecting youth.

# Conclusions and implications

## Including young people

A focus on youth issues is a relatively new dimension to urban regeneration policy and practice. The initiatives examined as case studies in this project are among the pioneers of the focus on youth. The extent of their achievement in including youth in regeneration, both in terms of addressing needs and involving young people, is modest but should be assessed within this pioneering context. Clearly, many aspects of programmes and projects, particularly those focused on empowering young people, are in their experimental stages.

Young people experience the difficulties of living in areas of multiple deprivation more acutely than many adults and more intensive programmes to address this disadvantage are justified. Young people also identify a distinctive set of concerns and priorities from adult decision makers which suggests a shift of emphasis is needed in traditional regeneration initiatives. Therefore, unless regeneration projects have a specific focus on youth, it is unlikely that young people's needs will be met by regeneration programmes and projects aimed at the general population. However, there is clear evidence in the case studies of a tension between foregrounding young people and compartmentalising youth issues. A number of the case studies demonstrate the dangers of assuming youth issues can be resolved by developing a small number of special initiatives. Our analysis suggests that, while projects and programmes targeted at young people's needs are necessary, they should be seen as part of a bigger whole.

The case study evidence is that urban regeneration initiatives are starting to take youth issues seriously. However, there remains a lot to learn about how young people's needs and concerns should be included in the content of regeneration initiatives and about how they can be involved in a meaningful way in regeneration structures and processes.

### Including young people's needs and concerns

Young people's expressed needs and concerns are being addressed only partially by regeneration initiatives. If regeneration was based centrally on young people's perspectives there would be:

- priority given to the quality of local leisure facilities;

- a greater emphasis on improving young people's relationship with adults living in the locality and, therefore, more projects designed to create intergenerational understanding;

- a shift from projects designed to improve employability to a focus on job creation;

- a focus on the image of the locality, with overcoming area-based discrimination an important objective;

- more attention given to young people over 20, who would not be written off as 'a lost cause';

- less emphasis on projects designed to contain or divert young people and more emphasis on policing practices;

- more focus on addressing young people's needs as young people and not only as future adults.

However, it would be wrong to focus solely on what young people say they want, and not to address the other aspects of their disadvantage, as outlined in Chapter 1. If regeneration schemes were based on young people's priorities alone, there would be little attention, for example, to health, homelessness and education.

Most regeneration schemes have not fully taken on young people's voiced concerns, nor tackled the range of material youth disadvantage. Instead, they have responded most readily to those needs which seem most closely connected to local economic competitiveness, including education, training and employability concerns. At the same time, they have picked up on some social concerns, expressed nationally and locally, about 'problem youth', and devised projects accordingly. Although several case studies adopted a well-integrated approach to young people's needs, this was seldom holistic.

## Including young people as active participants

Youth involvement in regeneration is necessary if initiatives are to address young people's own priorities. The finding of this study that there is a gap between adults' and young people's conceptions of their needs is evidence in itself of this. However, the current enthusiasm for giving youth a voice in regeneration has not yet been translated into mechanisms which allow this to happen effectively. Young people remain only minor players in urban regeneration decision making, if they are players at all. Further, their involvement has resulted mostly in marginal impacts on youth-specific issues and has had no impact on the wider regeneration agenda. There are four reasons for this.

*A tendency to seek simple solutions.* The attachment to youth forums in the case studies is an indicator of a tendency to oversimplify the complex issues involved in securing an effective youth voice. In particular, it typifies the tendency to focus on structures rather than facilitating processes. Youth participation works best when there is a range of channels and activities through which young people can engage with regeneration and when the importance of participation underpins the ethos of the initiative. Youth forums have tended to separate young people rather than integrate their perspectives with those of other players.

The research shows that youth forums are not the solution to securing effective youth participation, although they can play a useful role if they are well organised and resourced, and integrated into wider structures.

*Lack of clarity over purpose.* Three rationales underpin the contemporary support of youth involvement:

- to give young people a voice in decision making, allowing them to exercise their rights as 'fellow citizens', have their priorities addressed and, therefore, to develop a sense of ownership of the process of change;

- to act as a vehicle for the self-development of young people, through building confidence and skills and socialising them into the adult world;

- to train 'future citizens' about active citizenship.

In many cases, the three rationales were all apparent and in competition. The overt principal rationale was concerned with voice, but the reality was that the delivery (and modest impact) of youth participation projects tended to emphasise self-development, which then became the justification for the project. Indeed, this tendency was sometimes intensified by youth workers' traditional developmental agendas, and by regeneration professionals' interest in skills development and employability.

*Under-resourcing.* The level of resources allocated to youth involvement is, with a few exceptions, very low. This tendency to try to secure youth involvement on the cheap is linked to the drive to seek overly simple solutions.

*Ignoring the lessons of community participation.* Regeneration initiatives have largely failed to build on what is known about successful community involvement. In particular, the need to avoid having token representatives involved in partnership structures, without appropriate support or legitimacy, has been largely ignored. The lower expectations of youth involvement, reflected in inferior standards of governance regarding accountability of representatives to a wider body of youth people, and in the handpicking of youth delegates, minimises the potential impact of youth involvement on regeneration. Also, the lesson that people in powerful positions must adjust their language and behaviour so that the less powerful can make an impact has been set aside. That adults have to change in order to include young people is a key finding of the study.

Although the extent and impact of youth involvement was limited, there were some important elements of success among the case studies. The experience of youth involvement suggests it works most effectively when a range of participation mechanisms are in place. The mechanisms should:

- ensure young people have a share of power and influence by enmeshing youth participation mechanisms with urban regeneration decision making;

- provide opportunities for young people to speak on their own terms and territory;

- facilitate intergenerational contact and therefore help generate understanding.

Building effective youth involvement is a more difficult task than securing general community involvement and three issues need to be considered. First, the number of young people involved in formal decision making is tiny and is never likely to be large. Second, young people tend to lack the confidence and skills to participate fully in formal meetings. It should not be assumed that it is enough to have young people sitting around partnership tables – the atmosphere needs to be conducive to them making a contribution. Third, young people are more comfortable talking about many of their concerns within peer group settings, where they are in the majority. These three factors indicate that consultative mechanisms involving a broad group of young people should be developed in addition to participative mechanisms involving a few. Consultation is usually regarded as second best to participation, because the views expressed may be easily set aside, but ascertaining the views of young people in general is essential for devising appropriate action.

Finally, it is worth stressing that most young people are interested in having a say, but the level of enthusiasm and commitment varies enormously. The vast majority will give some time to consultation but only a few will give over their lives to the constant round of

meetings that is the lot of the professional volunteer. However, the case studies show that with the right support, and with incentives such as 'residentials', a greater number can become effective representatives contributing a moderate amount of their time to involvement.

### Conclusion

There is a common view that young people in disadvantaged areas are an alienated underclass, indeed some of the policy response has been driven by that perspective. The contacts made with young people in the course of this study suggest that that view is unfounded; they are not rejecting adults' general views and values, in fact, what they are seeking is adult respect and approval.

Urban regeneration initiatives have started to focus on young people, but there is still a lot to learn. The study suggests that they have a potentially important part to play in overcoming social exclusion among young people, and in developing more cohesive communities by focusing more closely on young people's material and expressed needs, and by uncovering common values and understanding between young people and older adults.

## Implications for urban regeneration policy

To a large extent, the findings of this report endorse the current direction of urban regeneration policy. Part of the reason that young people have started to come to the fore is the encouragement given to youth-focused projects under the SRB. The latest round of SRB initiatives, announced in Spring 1998, has a heavy weighting of schemes which focus entirely on young people, or which identify young people as the most important target group. So it seems that young people have been effectively moved up the agenda and are increasingly being included in regeneration.

Yet, without prejudging the new schemes, the experiences of many of our case studies suggests that young people can be too easily compartmentalised. They are considered to have different needs to older people, special 'youth workers' are required to run their projects, and the evidence shows that additional difficulties are faced in involving them in regeneration decision making. All this points to a 'special needs' approach. However, young people's needs are too important to be ghettoised. The welfare and economic position of youth, and their social behaviour, is critical to the overall well-being of the entire community. While the depth of youth disadvantage and the needs which are occasioned by the transition to adulthood are ample justification for special youth projects, these need to be seen as part of a holistic approach which regards young people as an integral part of society. In part this means not just focusing on the troubles of youth, but also on adults' approaches.

Some of our case studies had reasonably well-integrated, if not necessarily comprehensive, youth strategies where the youth element in regeneration was in itself logically programmed and fitted in well with an overall conception of a regeneration strategy. Others were far from this position. Few, if any, initiatives were located fully within an overall youth policy or strategy for the area. Current government policy favours attention to young people across a number of areas, notably employment (especially the 'New Deal'), crime (the Crime and Disorder Bill) and education, including the *Learning age* Green Paper. It seems likely that the focus on youth under SRB4 is a reflection of this overall policy direction, both in terms of regeneration partnerships making bids to suit the government's ideas, and the government responding in turn with agreement to fund those bids. It seems likely that the government's emerging policies will fill some of the important gaps we identified among current regeneration projects. 'New Deal' focuses on older young people, who were given little attention by our case studies; the promotion of the 'learning society' promises some attention to the educational (and not just the training) needs of young school leavers. On the other hand, it is likely that some aspects of the Crime and Disorder Bill, when enacted, will make relationships between the police and young people more difficult. The Bill rightly recognises the important problems that young people can cause in the community, but there are no policy measures which consider policing from the young persons' viewpoint, that is, the near universal experience of harassment.

While the new policies which seek to alleviate disadvantage among youth are to be welcomed, there is a potential problem in integrating the large number of initiatives aimed at young people coming through 'regeneration' routes and other sources. Our evidence is that policies and projects towards young people are often not well coordinated and, while we could not examine the impacts of individual projects, it seems likely that lack of synthesis will result in lower levels of effectiveness. All of this suggests that local authorities and regeneration partnerships need to develop youth strategies, encompassing as far as possible all agencies with some responsibility for young people's welfare.

The development of strategies usually requires forward assurance of funding. Until now regeneration budgets have been allocated on a firm one-off basis for a fixed period of time, usually five or seven years following a fairly short bidding period. While there is some room for manoeuvre, regeneration partnerships usually require to commit their funding at an early stage. In effect, a number of the more deprived areas have been able to develop a regeneration programme on the back of successive successful bids for challenge funding. However, the process is inevitably an uncertain one. The prospect of a rolling programme of regeneration funding, and a planning horizon of up to 10 years, discussed in the government's 1997 consultation paper *Regeneration programmes: The way forward* could have at least two benefits. First, it would allow initial capacity-building for young people to take place, and for young people's views then to feed into the specification of an overall strategy and sets of projects. Second, it would allow more reflection and flexibility in the development of strategies.

## Implications for local practice

To conclude we offer some practical suggestions for the main participants in regeneration projects, which are intended to help the more effective inclusion of young people.

*Regeneration practitioners and decision makers*

- Establish links to mainstream and other policies and programmes to ensure coordination and synergy and, therefore, maximum impact.

- Develop clarity over rationales, particularly over youth involvement.

- The timing of youth participation projects is a key issue. Schedule them early during the life of initiatives and, if possible, secure resources for capacity building before the initiative starts. But also recognise the importance of early action. Young people will keep their interest if they see the fruits of their labour early on.

- Resources and staffing are critical. There is a need for dedicated workers. Turnover within youth groups and the need for intense support must be recognised.

- Recognise that your ideas will be challenged by young people who have something worthwhile to say.

- Recognise that young people are motivated and looking for something challenging to do and keenly interested in what adults think of them.

- Think about how your language and procedures inhibit youth participation.

*Youth workers or dedicated support staff*

- Learn more about regeneration (it is different to youth work), in order to be able to support young people effectively.

- Recognise that youth forums are not the only answer to participation. Think through what is meant to be achieved by participation and find out how best to link youth participation into wider community and regeneration processes. Consider a range of mechanisms and structures.

- Learn about effective community participation and use its lessons to help develop more democratic and accountable structures for youth involvement.

- Provide young people with tailored training for regeneration. Mentoring can be highly effective.

*Community organisations*

- Attach more priority to young people's needs as young people and not only as 'citizens of the future'.

- Try to build links between generations and to develop structures which foster inclusion.

- Think about how your language and procedures inhibit youth participation.

*Young people*

- Learn from elsewhere how to get organised.

- Don't lose contact with your peer group.

- Think about the kinds of barriers you put up to adults, particularly through language.

# References

Atkinson, R. and Moon, G. (1994) *Urban policy in Britain: The city, the state and the market*, Basingstoke: Macmillan.

Black, C., Mayhew, P. and Percy, A. (1996) 'The 1996 British Crime Survey', *Home Office Statistical Bulletin*, 19.

DETR (Department of the Environment, Transport and the Regions) (1997) *Regeneration programmes – The way forward*, London: DETR.

Furlong, A. and Cartmel, F. (1997) *Young people and social change: Individualisation and risk in late modernity*, Buckingham: Open University Press.

Hickman, P. (1997) 'Is it working? The changing position of young people in the UK labour market', in J. Roche and S. Tucker (eds) *Youth in society: Contemporary theory, policy and practice*, London: Sage Publications.

Evans, A. (1996) *We don't choose to be homeless*, Report of the National Inquiry into Preventing Youth Homelessness, London: CHAR.

Lightfoot, J. (1990) *Involving young people in their communities*, London: Community Development Foundation.

Macfarlane, R. and Mabbot, J. (1993) *City Challenge: Involving local communities*, London: NCVO.

Roberts, K. (1997) 'Is there an emerging British "underclass": the evidence from youth research', in R. MacDonald (ed) *Youth, the 'underclass' and social exclusion*, London: Routledge.

West, P. and Sweeting, H. (1996) 'Nae job, nae future: young people and health in a context of unemployment', *Health and Social Care in the Community*, vol 4, pp 50-62.